THE SECRET
- OF -
REAL ESTATE
INVESTING

*The 8 Biggest Real Estate Beginner
Mistakes You Can Easily Avoid*

By Adell Paltrow

1

Disclaimer

advertising, and all other aspects of doing business in the US, Canada, or any other jurisdiction is the sole responsibility of the purchaser or reader.

ISBN: 9781698166025

Table of Contents

Introduction

The investment in the form of a real estate is on everyone's lips. Why? In the long term, real estate is a good investment alternative if interest rates are at as low a level as they are today. Will interest rates not rise again in the foreseeable future? Why should not we invest the money in stocks that promise much better returns than in the "good, solid property"?

Questions about questions that cannot be replied in general, the fact is, real estate investment is a good, conservative investment that some people can afford. There are very different facets of a real estate investment, which are a little bit more illuminated here.

One step ahead: Of course, this guide cannot replace an individual consultation. Inevitably, every human needs to decide for themselves which investment alternative fits him and also his desires.

The fact is that substantial consumers have used real estate ventures for many years. Which types of asset investment exist?

About

The real estate investment is based on the same principles as any other investment, that is to say, it consists of placing your money in a property or real estate to make a profit from rental income. The rental investment is unique in comparison with the other types of investment that the investor owner himself undertakes to calculate the profitability of his investment, whereas the financial institution is responsible for the investment.

If correctly done, the rental investment should allow the owner to build wealth in the long term. The investor also improves his purchasing power with his rental income. In another perspective, the rental investment is also made to provide real estate to his relatives. It also helps to ensure a roof since the owner can occupy the property can live when it comes time to retire.

The owner must keep an eye on various factors that affect the proper functioning of the rental. The geographical situation and the inventory are important elements that influence the value of the rental investment. You also require being aware of potential urban projects that can add value to the property if it is located in the area where it is planned.

There are many reasons to invest in rental real estate right now. The period is conducive to rental investment, while the risk is minimal. Other types of investment are much less accessible. Investing in equities is sometimes equivalent to playing at the casino, while bank investments offer a rather low return.

There is a downward trend in mortgage rates, and all indications are that the trend will continue after more difficult years. This aspect can vary according to the geographical zones, but everywhere the rates are low. The moment is therefore, conducive to investment. Also, the cost of real estate is low, which is an added benefit. The investor, therefore, has plenty of time to look for a property at a good price in a favorable sector to rent while making a small loan.

Another major reason to invest in rental real estate is the return. Once the loan has been repaid, the landlord receives the full rent. There are only long-term benefits. There are three types of profitability depending on the owner's objective: gross profitability, net profitability and profitability net of expenses. One more reason to take into consideration investing in real estate that the state supports the rental investment and also that lots of tax benefits are supplied to the property owner.

Chapter 1

What Is the Real-Estate

The property is a term defining and including any business or private related to real estate. The term commonly refers to the activities of management and transaction taking place on these properties, but it also touches on many related activities such as housing, construction, promotion, council, town planning, architecture, stewardship, etc. The law and finance are areas of activity essential to the functioning of the housing market.

We distinguish the movable property that can be moved from the real estate that cannot.

"Real estate" can, therefore, relate to:

- A land bare, that is to say without building (also called "land")
- A building or a part of a building, whatever the use (a building can have many uses: home, offices, storage, industrial or mixed-use).

We are talking about sales "real estate (date of creation 1920)" when the sale relates to a property. Only real estate items are normally included in a real estate sale.

The sale of the movable property must be carried out independently. In law, it is also considered that there are movable objects which can become real estate.

Thus, a tree in a transportable pot is a "mobile / furniture" object, while an earthen tree is "fixed / real estate," just like an independent brick becomes "building" as soon as it is incorporated into a building.

Inside the house, it can be seen that furniture can become "immovable" when for example, an unfurnished "kitchen furniture" becomes part of the real estate when it is hung on the wall. The furniture is said to have become "building by destination".

The 5 types of real estate investment

If you plan to get a property, there are multiple choices. Nonetheless, they might not all be ideal for you. That is why you have to take into account aspects such as your budget, expectations and also prompt demands.

1. Residential properties

It is the most timeless way to purchase the actual estate market; Buy areas to live, whether houses or apartments.

Among the benefits of this type of investment is that the demand - in a stable economic situation at the national level will increase, as the population continues to grow.

Also, Residential properties are usually more safeguarded versus exchange rate risks of local currencies, and the worth of the property will certainly expand over the years.

Now, the selection between residence or apartment will depend on what each buyer searches for according to their demands and expectations. For instance, it is different if you want to occupy it to live for a period with your family members than if you only mean to lease to foreigners.

2. Commercial properties

The purchase of commercial premises as well as workplaces is just one of the most dynamic sectors to make sure that it can give great earnings in the short-term, creates higher cash flow manufacturing contrasted to other realty investments.

It likewise has the possibility of having even more leases with certain kinds of commercial property.

It also has the possibility of having more leases with specific sorts of commercial property.

Commercial property investors, along with having the necessary resources, have likewise to have suitable techniques, for instance, great networking, prompt guidance, and also a financial expectation.

3. Industrial properties

This point consists of all those spaces that are used for commercial objectives. One of the favorable aspects of this financial investment is that it can be made use of for numerous usages, either as a storage facility or as a workplace, to create items or services. You can likewise segment and rent the subspaces that are generated.

4. Retail properties

In Chile for example, the building and construction of the shopping mall do not reduce. Currently, only in the Metropolitan Region, there go to the very least 5 large tasks. There are a lot more stores and brands, which creates a higher need for these areas.

In this property choice, we need to take into consideration variables such as distribution or place. The latter can affect the success of the property since in some cases the level of sales counts on the selection of individuals traveling with that field.

5. Real estate investment funds

Property Investment Funds or Real Estate Investment Trust (REIT), are those investment firms that have real estate assets and that obtain revenue generally from the leases of the same. In these cases, they provide shares on the Stock Exchange, like other companies that are listed on the supply market.

In this situation, capitalists add the quantity necessary to get, create, and handle the property. Its revenues are dispersed as rewards.

One of the benefits of this method is that the financier can swiftly offer the shares (or quotas) if he requires liquidity and also the investment in property funds enables buying industrial as well as houses.

A deep study must be done that includes aspects such as the dimension of the fund, a reduced degree of debt, the amount and also high quality of the investors, etc

Chapter 2

The Myths and Realities That You Need To Know About Real Estate Investment

Remember that investing in real estate is buying real estate that generates income or is intended for investment purposes as a place of residence that is, house, an apartment or in some cases, land.

The usual thing is for investors with real estate experience to have several real estate properties, one of which is the main residence, while the others are used to generate income through leasing and profits through the adjustment of prices.

Now, if you are not sure about what is true and what is a myth when it comes to investing in property, we give you some tips and steps to follow so that you can take this important step.

3 Myths about Investing In Real Estate

1. You need a huge capital

the perfect point for any person who wishes to purchase property is to have sufficient capital to stay clear of having to require financing. However, to buy a property, you should always have some initial capital. For this, you have two ways, cash or through a mortgage.

The preceding suggests that it is not necessary to be rich to build an empire of properties, but there are risks associated with the loan of money since you must ensure sufficient income in the future lease to cover the costs of the mortgage.

2. Now is not the best time.

Thinking that you should wait until the real estate market improves is another of the most common myths about real estate investment.

It is never a hard time to start getting residential properties while using the right technique, considering both external and also inner factors that affect the decision.

In external factors, one should consider the economic health of the country, be sure that interest rates are low or that the economic rebound of the local economy is stable.

Internal factors are compromised when the purchase of a property responds to an impulsive act, or there is not enough capital, so the risk of losing a good opportunity is even greater.

3. Rental income covers all costs

Some investors assume that the rental income will cover the value of the mortgage and a little more; that is, they will generate a profit practically without effort.

However, the cost of maintaining the property must be taken into account; unless a rent income more significant than the mortgage payment is obtained. To confirm that the investment will be energetically profitable, calculate if the value of the lease will be equal to or greater than all the monthly expenses involved. Otherwise, it would be unlikely that rental income covers all costs.

It is necessary to check the property regularly to keep it in good condition, pay the corresponding taxes and have a good lease contract that allows protecting the owner against future tenants.

3 Real Estate Investment Realities

1. The administration of properties is key in the real estate investment

It is a very important point to avoid problems with the tenants. Delivering the administration of the property or properties to a specialized company brings many advantages since they are responsible for evaluating those who seek to lease your property.

Companies dedicated to property management have rating systems that allow locating potential tenants according to certain levels of risk. Also, they have the experience to make lease agreements with clauses that protect the owner and the tenant.

2. Property management is a long-term process

If you are going to take the train of investment in real estate, it is important to consider that it is not a financial miracle overnight.

The investor should formulate a business plan with realistic goals and strive to achieve the objectives every day. The process of investment and administration in real estate is indeed slow and will take time. However, all hard work will pay off, and a life of financial freedom and independence will begin to materialize.

The key is to invest time and energy in acquiring the correct knowledge in real estate investment.

3. Investing is an easy strategy to monetize

If the investor for some reason is in financial difficulties or wants to invest in something else, it will always be effortless to sell the property or properties acquired, or mortgage them to obtain a loan.

Investing in real estate translates, finally, into an open option to acquire other similar or better investments. If the owner of a property wants to invest in something of greater value, he will always have the advantage of selling or being an endorsement for other investments; an aspect that banks appreciate a lot.

In short, investment in real estate is a great business opportunity. The important thing is to have clarity and knowledge before investing money and time in it.

Therefore, the key is to work intelligently and not make decisions hastily or on a whim.

Investigate the real estate strategy and the type of property before deciding is another factor that cannot be left behind, and mainly, be up to date with market conditions. What worked last year may not work currently.

However, we must not be afraid. Successful real estate investors think nimbly and modify their strategy according to the conditions of the real estate market. For this reason, the importance of continually studying, receiving advice and reading articles about the real estate world is the key.

The two best options to pay the foot of a future property

Nowadays, to buy a property, the idea is to have enough savings to finance part of the property and thus pay for the rest with a mortgage loan. Many people do so, saving foot money on investment instruments such as term deposits and conservative mutual funds, which are known as insurance but not very profitable.

However, a practice that is gaining more followers is to pay the foot of a property with future delivery, in installments, to reduce the possibility of over-indebtedness.

In the best of cases, and if the investor has good savings capacity, this alternative includes acquiring a property in white or green to save money during the construction phase of the building, and thus finish paying the fees of the foot in the date or a few months before the delivery of the property.

Thus, the payment of the foot is not coupled with the dividend of the mortgage loan. Acquiring properties by the promise of purchase in white or green are two attractive investment options due to its high profitability. These acquisition approaches are easier than depositing monthly in a time down payment, shared fund or a savings account considering that it is an investment in UF and also subject to the resources gain of construction.

1. Why buy a property in green?

Buying in green is the promise of buying a home that is under construction. Therefore, it is not yet finished nor does it have the definitive reception granted by the corresponding municipality.

Since not all people have enough savings to pay the foot off immediately, among the most attractive advantages of buying in green is flexibility in foot payment. Being a property with a delivery delay, a single term is granted in the real estate market to save this money and pay it in installments.

Thus, the capitalist pays the foot during the months that postpone the function of the job, which typically varies between 12 and 30 months.

The benefits of purchasing in green include: Good value to buy cheap in a good neighborhood. Buying in green finally becomes around business for real estate investors looking to buy less expensive in a more expensive neighborhood, then lease or sell at a higher price

Being an advance purchase, the future owner has more freedom of choice in the department he wants to buy, such as location, connectivity and neighborhood conditions.

Another positive aspect to consider is that the green building pilots are usually available when the projects finish, so any advantage is also that having an idea of how the building is made can be negotiated to make adjustments or modifications.

However, investing the foot in this option has **two disadvantages:**

Time. You cannot dispose of the property immediately. Buying in green implies a wait from months to years, although from the economic point of view it usually turns out to be much more convenient than doing it under the modality of purchase with immediate delivery.

It is important to be clear that the date on which the real estate agents commit to deliver the department often changes in days, weeks and even months. Everything will depend on the conditions and efficiency of the work or, even, budgetary problems.

A blind purchase. Being an advance purchase, you cannot see what is being paid, since there are no drivers available at the time of signing.

Although it is not typical to occur, the result might differ; there are inconsistencies between what is offered and also the fact of the property, such as common areas: stockrooms, bbq areas, pool or car park lots.

To avoid bad times, it is best to save the strategies and also specs provided at the time of acquisition. In case of differences in the shipment of the property, it is suggested to settle the problem directly (or through a representative) with the actual estate before reaching other circumstances.

2. What is the purchase of blank properties?

Acquiring properties in white is when the project currently has the due permission of the structure or competence of the land, but the excavations have not yet begun.

That is to claim, not only is a home or home acquired before its building is finished; however the documents are authorized before the

job also begins.

The actual estate supplies a pledge of an approximate time when the new job will undoubtedly be offered. The investor only understands the plans as well as details on paper that show exactly how it will certainly be adjusted in the structure.

The process of delivery of the property takes two years or more. However, the blank value is much lower than the green mode or immediate delivery.

The main **advantages** of buying in white are:

Economic. The purchase price is reduced and grants facilities in foot payment. If the interested party does not have the total value of the foot, the property is fragmented into installments until the delivery deadline.

Flexibility. When buying in white, the client can choose the preferred locations of the property, such as distribution, parking, and warehouse.

The necessary thing to keep in mind when acquiring under this modality is that since it is an earlier acquisition than its green version, both the economic benefits and also the negative aspects of acquiring blindly are even a lot more intensified. To not take big surprises, the most advisable thing is to choose a reliable real estate, and that offers you the best price.

The best alternative to purchase properties is to pay the fee in installments, in green or white. Nevertheless, not all individuals have adequate savings to pay the foot quickly or are not yet qualified in banking, so it becomes essential to take into consideration other options to save as well as produce passion with time.

To accomplish this, there is a valid option to purchase the foot of a property: invest in common funds. It contains a somewhat a lot more dangerous investment modality. It is a sort of investment where the amounts do not have assured income given that they involve the threat that the financial investments improvised not provide the anticipated return.

Mutual funds are the number of payments in cash supplied by individuals and also legal entities to a company or manager controlled by the Commission for the Financial Market (CMF).

When delivering this money to the administration firm, it spends it on various types of economic tools that are safe and securities of public offering or items, with the function of getting a profit that will be dispersed among all those who added. It should be clear that investing the cash to a manager is a danger that must be borne by each factor of the chosen mutual fund.

The intriguing thing about this kind of real estate investment is that it is feasible to demand information on the historical earnings of the chosen mutual fund, in order to compare it with success gotten by other funds of the same type and in equal durations of time, or with the earnings of various additional financial savings and investment alternatives.

By doing this, you can make a much better decision and also stay clear of future threats.

If the risk surpasses the resistance of the financier, the financier can request the rescue of the investment changed by the success that has experienced the whole, or part of it, which will be paid in a period no higher than that established by the interior laws of the fund, which can not be greater than 10 days after the withdrawal demand has been made.

The pledge of purchase for genuine estate in white or green will certainly always be the most effective choice, for the opportunity of paying in interest-free installments.

The payment of the foot in cash justifies only if paying in installments involves paying high interest.

Both cash and in installations are appealing financial investment choices because of their possible productivity and are extra convenient than regular monthly down payment in a term deposit, shared fund or an interest-bearing account.

The funds count as a legitimate financial investment choice, however with a reduced but liquid return.

Chapter 3

Will you lose money in real estate?

It might seem weird for an investor to claim this, yet you can lose money on residential or commercial property. As well as there are a variety of ways in which this is possible-- a few of them evident as well as many concealed.

Usually, even more houses sell at a loss than residences, more financiers cost a loss than owner inhabitants, more local homes sell at a loss than those in the city. We require digging further into the data to offer some reasons for these differentials. However, the critical takeaway below is that the saying "risk-free as homes" is misinforming.

Currently, this information only considers the price. It does not consider acquiring expenses, holding costs, renovation expenses, interest costs, marketing prices. So it doesn't count a lot of other residential or commercial properties that have lost money. It likewise does not tally up the quantity of home not being marketed that is currently worth less than their owners spent on it! How do you even determine that?

Below are some methods you can quickly lose money on property:

1. You pay too much at the optimal of the marketplace

When the market is warm, purchasers panic and also frequently pay way too much. If you ignore the negatives of a property in your rush to obtain onto the market, you could end up purchasing a property that decreases in worth, even while others rise.

2. You lose cash since you fail to identify significant opportunities

When the marketplace reduces, people state, "we'll wait to see if prices drop". Smart investors make the most of a buyers' market and also have the confidence to secure the quality property at reasonable rates. A few of those that purchased quickly upload the GFC reaped gains in a short period.

3. You get cheated by a property spruiker

My heart breaks when I become aware of individuals succumbing to the spin of "financial investment experts". Lots of capitalists who have gotten in local areas (believe mining towns, for circumstances) and new growths in smaller cities have unknowingly been sold a loser. Numerous retired life desires have been shattered by doing this.

4. You go after amount over quality

One depressing instance is the young couple who have crowned '2012 UNITED STATES's property Investor of the Year' by Your Property Investment Magazine after obtaining a profile of 16 residential properties over 5 years. Only 3 brief years later on, they created on their site, "we owe in extra of $5.8 million on property worth $2.3 million".

5. Poor property choice

It's owner-occupiers who raise prices, as they are most likely to be more emotional than investors. It stands to factor that if you purchase a residential property that just interest financiers, your chance for funding development is limited. However, if you stop working to comprehend what functions are preferred with regional customers, you will undoubtedly lose money compared to the gains you could make with the more appealing property.

6. The wrong area

Some areas use lasting growth, others are up as well as coming, yet others remain in various phases of the home cycle. Property financial investment is a long video game, and also the selection of areas needs to think about long-term goals and appetite for danger. Investigating demographics and also where framework projects are happening is not enough; you require to recognize micro-environmental consider an order to stay clear of a place where you might lose money.

Why People still Investing in Real Estate

The purchase of a home usually comes from a need, from fulfilling the need or desire to own a home, and not so much from the perspective of investment. Part of the population views physical real estate as a pure investment, in the form of investment property. For example, real estate as an investment category has many facets. Institutional investors, for example, make a distinction between offices, commercial spaces, hotels, etc. Let us therefore briefly explain the different motives and ways of investing in real estate.

Good Reasons

Anyone who regards real estate as an investment must analyze it as such: what are the building blocks of the expected return?

Relatively stable price evolution

Over the past 40 years, the Belgian house price index, compiled by 'Bank for International Settlements' (BIS), has risen from 13.55 at the end of 1973 to 144.88 at the end of 2013. This results in an average price increase of around 6 percent per year. Residential real estate equals the price performance of shares and bonds. In addition to a similar return in the long term, real estate, on the other hand, is experiencing a less volatile price evolution in the short term. Since investors have an aversion to short-term fluctuations, they are particularly attracted by the attractive risk-weighted return on real estate.

Current income

If you are looking for investment not only for 'value retention', but also for recurring income, you have found the right place with real estate. On the revenue side, we find potential value increases and rental income. On the cost side, there are all kinds of transactions, maintenance, financing costs and possible decreases in value. The rental of residential and commercial properties generates an income stream that offers protection against inflation even with stable property prices since rental income is regularly indexed.

Capital investments in real estate are usually financed with debt. If you deduct the interest charges and other operational costs, such as for the maintenance of the buildings, from the rental income, you will receive the net income stream or the return on the investment in real estate. For a well-located building, you can count on an annual return of 3 to 4 percent. This is even more apparent than the current average coupon interest on bonds or the average dividend yield on shares.

Incorrect reasons

The sustainable price increase of real estate is mainly due to the fundamental functioning of supply and demand. Unbridled optimism sometimes causes people to invest in real estate for the wrong motivation. We illustrate this based on two examples.

"House prices only go up."

Not only in Belgium but also worldwide are the demand for real estate increasing due to the increasing population, while the supply of arable land is limited. As a result, the long-term trend in real estate prices remains focused. However, as investors, you should not enter into a brash mind. Just like on the stock market and the bond market, there are times of overvaluation, stagnation and bursting bubbles on the real estate market. It is therefore important to take account of short-term shocks within the long-term trend. For example, puncturing the real estate bubble in the United States created new opportunities.

Holiday homes: investing versus enjoying

For an investment in a temporary stay, it is also necessary to look at the long-term return and to compare it with other investments (e.g., shares). Buying a holiday home is nice to enjoy but not always a good investment. When the price of your holiday home drops then you have also lost money. Just think of Spanish holiday homes that have fallen sharply in recent years.

Moreover, such a stay entails relatively many costs, such as extra maintenance costs. Regarding the expected return, you also have to make a comparison for other holiday homes with other long-term investments. A holiday home that you enjoy but that does not yield is not an investment but an (expensive) hobby. If you want to invest to achieve maximum returns, there are better alternatives.

How can you invest in real estate?

For the average private investor, real estate often turns out to be synonymous with tangible bricks. For many, buying their own home means their first and only participation in real estate. After all, paired with mortgage financing, purchasing a family home is a tax efficient way of saving and one of the few ways in which individuals can invest with leverage through debt financing.

Belgium, therefore, has a strong tradition of real estate ownership. But real estate ownership often implies high transaction costs, such as for the broker, notary, and registration. Moreover, real estate is illiquid, highly concentrated (large amount invested in a single property) and owners usually underestimate maintenance costs. Do you want to diversify part of your assets by investing in real estate? Then you have two alternative investment options:

Real estate investment trusts

Property investment funds are professional managers of real estate. For example, some property investment funds specialize in retirement homes, while others pursue a more diversified property policy. List their shares on the stock exchange. To qualify as a property investment fund on the Brussels stock exchange, real estate companies must, among other things, pursue a debt ratio of up to 65 percent and pay at least 80 percent of their net rental income as a dividend to shareholders. These conditions are also attractive to investors. Also, the market price of the property investment fund largely follows the price evolution of the underlying assets. By, among other things, comparing the price with the net book value, you can judge whether the share of the property investment fund is cheap or expensive.

SICAVs

SICAVs are traditional investment funds that invest in real estate and property managers. These investment funds are not listed on the stock exchange and are therefore not bound by the corresponding qualification conditions. However, through funds, you can invest more liquid and from small amounts in real estate. In this way, your total family assets are also less concentrated in an individual investment. SICAVs also have a broader investment perspective than SICAVs, which are usually anchored locally. These investors, therefore, offer investors the opportunity to respond to the development of the real estate market abroad with a small investment.

Chapter 4

Why real estate: advantages

You're not going to believe it, but it's much more substantial than injecting money into the stock market. Thanks to the investment in real estate you can achieve an added value when reselling the purchased property, invest for a peaceful retirement, and also for your children.

The added value is the fact that you sell the purchased goods at an amount greater than the one you bought it from. Taxes exist to regulate your profit, but there is still a profit to be made. What is very interesting is that your capital gain is exempt from all taxes in cases such as the resale of a building to an amount below or equal to $15 000, the resale of a building that you held during more than 30 years old, when the reseller is an invalid or receives an old age pension.

If you care about how to manage your retirement, invest in rental real estate for example. These can be modern or traditional apartments, townhouses or student houses. By choosing, for example, to invest in credit, you do not exhaust your wallet. Because renting the property allows you to repay and earn more. These incomes will enable you to have a better situation during retirement.

By investing in real estate through a loan, you can benefit your family. Indeed, if it is rental investment, after your death the family will keep the apartment since your loans are protected by insurance: that of death-disability. The refund is taken care of, and your family will always receive the rent. The reduction coefficients are granted to you and your family, as long as you do not rent an apartment to your children or family members.

Tax laws that benefit

When you invest in new rental, a tax reduction of 21% is achievable with the support of the law Pinel, over 20 years. An 11% tax reduction is possible if you rent a furnished apartment (Censi-Bouvard law). You can also recover up to 20% on VAT depending on your status. Similarly, significant reductions are granted, if you rehabilitate an old building, but in protected areas, and which you own (the Malraux law). And if you buy a house classified MH, the Historic law Monument offers you a more tax.

Success in real estate

Leverage, potential appreciation, returns are other things you need to know to excel in real estate investing.

Leverage is the least drain on your stock market and makes it easy for you to invest in real estate. It involves borrowing money (in a bank perhaps) to invest. The investment does not cost you anything. Because it will be your tenants, who will pay the rent, after the refund all the rest will be yours. Just make sure you have a quality building.

The gain is your first gain if you resell your property. Generally, reselling the purchased good make you pocket a lot of money if you manage the transaction well. The resale amount is always higher than the purchase price even though the representative value of housing has increased by more than 8% per year since 1900 in the French region.

Rental real estate investment yields between 1 and 10%. There are many unfounded controversies around this performance. But you have to realize that, even in the case of a loan to start, your tenants help you a lot to repay. The rent collected at the end of each month is a guarantee for you to pay off your loans. Also, your return will reach 100% if you can find a 100% investment.

Some steps to enjoy his investment in real estate

First, be sure to buy your property at a moderate price. Do not buy it too much. Because the future of the market could surprise you. In this, find a seller who is ready to sell. To buy at a better price, look for a seller who does not control the market and who is not an expert in real estate.

Second, find a good location for your good. To help you find a better location, search the internet, newspapers, etc. If you find a proper positioning for your building, you will easily find tenants who will pay well, because they will see a utility to reside in your good. Indeed, an excellent location will make the area will be very attractive. Mainly because of the presence of infrastructures, schools, administrative buildings, market, etc.

Third, buy in your area and consider installing a work team. Pay a property in the locality where you reside yourself, avoid expensive trips and respond in a short time in case of emergency. While creating a team such as an accountant, a real estate agent and a notary makes it easy for you. Indeed, one or the other can answer according to the type of problem which you meet in your real estate project. Similarly, having a real estate agent at your side, you focus your energy on specific tasks.

Real estate can be a solution for you to your various concerns. Why real estate? Because it has incalculable advantages to ensure you a good retirement, to reduce your taxes, to assure the future of your family, etc. Also, several laws currently in force facilitate investment in real estate.

Is real estate a good investment?

The home is usually a good investment for retirement. But should you buy rented real estate as a financial position?

Brokers currently often promise property yields between 4 and 6 percent. Sounds quite good in times when there is not much to get with interest rate products. But do these numbers agree?

No, not anymore. Such returns come from a time when you could buy real estate at the price of 20 times net rent. But today you pay 25- or even 30-fold. This is true at least for the big cities if you want to buy a property as a yielding object, but it depends just not on the price. You also have to ask yourself: how much rent cans I take? If the apartment is already rented, you cannot increase arbitrarily. And at new leases, we have a rental price brake at least in all major cities. New buildings are excluded. But if you buy something used and not wholly modernized, it is true. If someone speaks of 5 percent return, I think that's pretty unrealistic.

What can go wrong?

There may be rent losses or unplanned costs, especially in old buildings. Also, demand could decline again in the future. In general, you have a real estate investment as a so-called lump risk. You tie no small amounts, but a few hundred thousand euros capital. If you have them lying around - good. Most buyers have to borrow a bit. Then it is important to get rid of these debts quickly. At least three percent repayment should be made anyway with every mortgage lending. But if the buyers are traveling with one or two percent repayment, they are already taking a high risk. I would say: The property is quite difficult as an investment. And it has not become easier.

Why not?

Because real estate has become expensive, in the 7 essential cities, residential property costs increased by virtually 50 percent between 2010 and 2015. Rents have additionally climbed greatly, yet not to that level.

And then the question is how the price trend goes on. Who should buy the property later? At the moment, demand is high because the loans are so cheap. But at some point, the interest will rise again. Then the potential buyers have to spend more on financing again. Many will prefer to invest their equity elsewhere. The potential buyers are likely to decline, and prices will come under pressure, especially for existing real estate.

Suppose I have a new building in a perfect location. Am I at least on the safe side with that?

If you get the new building also cheap, the prospects are good. But then all three criteria have to be fulfilled. When it comes to situation, of course, the question arises, whether in 10 or 15 years will be even good. What does public infrastructure look like? Are there good transport connections, shopping facilities, and secondary schools? The latter is important, especially if you are building for families.

For families? I thought single apartments are so much in demand. Should not you instead invest in them?

Yes and no. This is supported by the fact that rents are rising faster, so it pays off faster. But singles are moving more often. So you have higher vacancies and renovations.

However, I would recommend somewhat of specific property instead get an entire apartment or condo structure considering that you can also coordinate with other individuals. You can split the expense and also usually can additionally get reduced costs.

Before you leave a few hundred thousand euros on the money account, you prefer to invest in a cheap apartment in a good location. But that is not a self-runner. And you should say goodbye to profit expectations like five percent or more.

Chapter 5

7 Sources of Realty Investing Failing

1. Quitting Too Soon

- In real estate, firstly, a lot of beings give up ahead of time. I see it where they obtain some impetus, they collect takes place going.

- But there's an epidemic nowadays in its very own country, where it was recognizing what's occurring with business like Groupon or Facebook as well as they make sure the kind of funds that can be developed with some of these design firms, and they assume that equates to every various other small company in America, as well as it precisely doesn't.

What occurs is they don't generate income in the very first few months and they terminate, they surrender.

- Now they might not claim they're providing or quitting up.

- They may make use of certain self-justifications like," Well, I really did not see results," or this is a good one," Well, this is not an excellent use my day since I've got a new opening that's also much better."

- I call that the yard is a continuously greener syndrome, where people are always looking for something various and fresh after a couple of months. It doesn't work.

- You've seen this when people take place diet plans or beings attempt to obtain health as well as those examples. It's extremely comparable. A ton of money of beings quit too early.

Stay with It

I submit to you that if you obtain active in your market as well as you begin to figure out that the other oppositions are in your neighborhood ball that is additionally real estate investing, that the bulk of them in two years will no longer exist, in five years you'll possibly be the only one if you're continuing it out, as well as ideally you're very successful. The majority of beings are so transient, whether it's real estate or anything. A couple of individuals can exactly stick to it lasting. That's where the power play is. The longer you're in, the even more success is. If you do not ... If you succumb to any one of the various other 7 I'm about to share with you, if you precisely do this one, you'll prosper. I indicate if it takes you 25 years, if you adhere to it long sufficient, you'll look at some point figure it out. The amount 1 mode that beings stop working in real estate is they retire. Pretty straightforward.

2. Ran Out of Funds

It seems pretty obvious. Well, lacking money is not just not having accessibility to cash for a deal.

It's not able to feed yourself as well as you need to go on and proceed to another thing. It's getting aroused concerning a chance than not having the capacity to stick it out long sufficient for points to start to make feeling.

I made this blunder in the begin. I quit my job and started the property business full day. At the same time, I did not have any funds and a lack of cash. I was enduring my truck, consuming on beans. These are terrible ideas.

A little bit of funds relocates a lengthy method in real estate. If you're in there long enough, fantastic points are going to take place. Does that make feeling?

3. Make Poor Deals

This set clangs easy enough." Okay, yeah, I get it Adell, so I stopped working since I did a bad bargain."

It's a whole lot a lot more hard to state no to a spate than it is to claim yes, specifically if you're in a scenario where you need to make a deal cultivate due to the fact that perhaps you obtained begun in this and also produce your spouse, considerable various other, moms, and dad, pal, relative, somebody is journeying your heart and also they're stating," Well, you're not making anything take place. I have not even heard you do a wave yet." You get anxious, and you begin hopping on spates that aren't that excellent offers.

Usually, the reason reduced offers take place is either

- a) you do not recognize what you're doing, or

- b) Even worse, you're anxious, you have to have an offer happen.

- Maybe you're on this entire day and you need a spate to project to make sure that you can maintain your rehabilitation staff active. I've seen that in the past. That's just outrageous.

What takes actual smarts is being able to say no, especially when the spate is open. If you're active as well as possibly you've got opposition in the area and maybe you're looking at a wave and also some other objections are, I've seen where people dictation up precisely to complete and drum their oppositions. Silly. Every wave has to base on its own 2 paws. Doing poor deals very, very easy setting to fail as well as come a cropper.

4. Poor Choice in Partnership

This is remarkably typical. There are some superb the benefit of is offered on collaboration agreements or partnership agreements like style where you've obtained greater than one event about the spate and they both introduce substantial amounts of worth. The trouble is what lots of people do is they go out, particularly if they're all new since anxious and also they're brand-new, as well as it's brand name brand-new in service sectors, it's obtained somewhat of an unfortunate name.

I mean, should be considered it, when "you're telling" close friends or family members at an alcoholic drink event," Hey, I'm most likely to be an investor." Oh, one of those we get lives beings." It does not seem all that eye-catching and also exciting. What occurs is to buffer someone's confidence a great deal of day they'll become grab organisation companions, buddy, somebody else to generate, so that they can both be doing it with each other. Well, that's usually a terrible idea. I have listened to many great friendships, lifelong rapports bust-up over one bad real estate spate.

Examples

The 2 individuals that fabricated large-hearted surge searching. I will not use their epithets; however these 2 people they produced what's currently this exceptionally popular brag. Those 2 people did a real estate wave together to buy some nation near among these motions shatters, one of this luck, and also it expanded badly; therefore, they don't chat any longer.

Another example, the people I utilized to invest the vacations with, with their very own family members, is likely to be 3 households. 3 different families would spend with each other on the holidays. Well, not their family members, but the various other 2 tenants, they did a real estate together. Spoiled. Boom, they no more talk. These beings, we invested holidays together for 20 years, no more talk, rumbling. 2 the team of pals of the quarry from college. They graduated from university, and they started doing waves. One was an attorney. One was a contractor. The attorney attracted the cash. The specialist did the renovation cultivate. One wave extended the poor, and they never chatted once again. They have been partners considering that they were kids. I mean, I can continue and on. The bad partnership is such a toxic happen. It takes place regularly.

What's the Solution?

Just make partnership contracts if the partner is returning a significant amount of value, either unbelievable tradition, fund, or both, or only something that you don't have. That's vital. You also require to know precisely what is going on with existing collaboration, when's it comes to an end. I see a lot of beings do not obtain wed "I ve been considering" exactly how they're going to get divorced. In an organisation partnership, you need to know precisely how points end.

Since what most individuals do is they grab someone that recognizes as little or little concerning real estate as they do, and they do it for the objectives of an uncertain period collaboration and happens to fall apart. It's most likely taking place to you right currently, some of you watching. I'm just preparing light to the truth; this is a very severe circumstance that you might be going via.

5. Larger and also Better Deals

You stopped, ran out of money, you do poor offers, poor collaboration. However, there's even more. I call it big as well as much more practical ideas. I'll claim big as well as much more effective bargains.

Well, another amusing idea that occurs is that often, people are successful. Then they run," Well, if I achieve success at this, I can do huge waves and also I can do big waves." What the hell is do is they leave their bread and even butter that's become aware fantastic coin and that's killing it and also doing fantastic and they go up and also they try massive and also much more effective waves, as well as they go into something that they know little or absolutely nothing about, and even in the end the entire thought drops apart. I can tell you all type of company stories, both real estate as well as in the organisation globe where someone has a golden goose, something that's very successful, yet they obtain burnt out with it or whatever as well as they wish to do something also more significant and they go onto that as well as they fall short every little thing. You might know somebody that's gone through. There's an expression that's been made use of in some service journals revealed stay with your knitting, remain with your knitting, where you stay with what's functioning.

As you find I stay with my knitting, I rehearse what I proclaim. I'm a residential real estate. I am doing the comfortable single-family house apartment, and duplex triplex quadruplet, simple residential trash I've been doing for times as well as years and times and also times. Beings ask me regularly," Adell, do you do these big industrial waves now?" No, I stay with my knitting, because I recognize it makes in the dough.

6. Obtaining Lucky

Right here's an intriguing one. You get fortunate. This is most likely to comply with the last one too.

This can be harmful since what can occur is you can do your very first deal and also make a killing. What ends up happening is you obtaining luck provided you a false-hearted feeling of safety and even you end up falling apart in the following pair of waves.

Obtaining good luck is an extremely, really large factor why people fall short in real estate. It's because they get this false-hearted feel of fact where they think they were the ones in charge of that success, where the recommendation is had absolutely nothing to do with them.

7: You Don't Know What You're Doing

Do not understand what you're doing. , if you were obtaining started in real estate, hopefully you are attempting to accumulate some educational level. "you've got an issue".

You will be facing 2 difficulties.

- The very first trouble is this. You might have a problem with capability absorption.

- What does that symbolize? That plans the capacity for you to retain the info you're finding out.

What happens to a lot of individuals is as they distance themselves away from institution year after year after year, they offer their brain on car pilot in a lot of methods, and also their mind doesn't obtain exerted. The mind is simply a muscular tissue. Then, even more you use it, the best it receives, the stronger it gets, the extremely ideal it accesses being rapid, at absorbing thoughts. It likewise pertains to your diet plan, your initiative, all kind of things contribute in your ability to soak up expertise, particularly smart knowledge, right stuff that's most likely to make you efficient in life.

The very first problem

Even if you have accessibility to excellent knowledge, if you've ever been in a circumstance where you seem like people need to inform you something 30 experiences for it to embed that brain, it indicates you reached begin activity this thing some even more. Currently, outside of having a legit clinical subject the most fabulous idea you can do is exert your mind by expending it. That will make a big difference.

Problem 2: Identifying Good Information

What's going to lead you astray? I send to you that the majority of things that you're going to enjoy, you're going to check out, you're going to listen to, a lot of it is sick.

There are various dispositions that the information the company has.

Possibly they sell complete items, so their angle is to inform you regarding a certain metropoli and why currently is the best time to buy in that metropolis because of the work, etc. Well, that can be done because they're selling the property.

Possibly it's a real estate like lecturer tutor guru that is in fact hasn't been associated with the real estate organisation in a long time, however they've gotten genuinely efficient offering. So maybe they're just offering their info.

Maybe they're just reworking old-fashioned stuff.

This is the worst, possibly they have all of the most excellent functions, but they are incorrect.

Possibly they're efficient their neighborhood domain for granted, yet there's still inaccurate. You need to be able to find the signal.

It's effortless for that to occur since there's so much understanding out there coming at you from so several various dispositions. That's easier stated than done since that intends, wide range 1 you've obtained to discover the signal, the absolute truism, the most excellent expertise out there, wide range 2, you've obtained to be able to absorb it.

The issue is what a lot of people do is they go out, specifically if they're brand name brand-new, because anxious and also they're brand-new, and it's brand name brand-new in service industries, it's got somewhat of a negative name.

I know a lot of beings do not get married "ve been believing regarding" how they're going to obtain separated. I can inform you all kinds of service tales, both real estate as well as in the organisation globe where someone has a cash cow, something that's hugely effective, but they obtain bored with it or whatever and also they want to do something too more significant and also they go onto that and they fall short whatever. The more you use it, the extremely best it obtains, the more powerful it gets, the very best it captures at being speedy, at soaking up ideas. That's easier claimed than done because that intends, plethora 1 you've obtained to discover the signal, the obvious truism, the best knowledge out there, multitude 2. You've got to be able to absorb it.

Chapter 6

Common Mistake Those Real Estate Investors Always Make

Ten essential points to check before investing in real estate, and as many mistakes to avoid

1,The environment and location of the property

One of the most important criteria for investing in rental real estate, as important as the size of the property and the variety of bedrooms.

Why?

Because it will only define your possibilities to exploit it and then to resend it

Here are the factors likely to influence your choice on the location and the environment of your future real estate acquisition:

The situation: fundamental for investing in rental real estate

The safety, the quality of life and the education of the children - if your tenants have some -depend mainly on the environment in which they live. The choice of tenants will therefore logically take into account this data.

Another point not to neglect: the state of the surrounding buildings.

Dilapidated and abandoned buildings could lead to severe nuisances in the future, and discourage tenants while compromising your resale opportunities at a reasonable price

The same is true of buildings typified social housing of excellent quality.

The geographic location

The apartment that is your potential rental investment is it close to major centers of life? (Hospital, big employers ...)

- Public transport nearby?
- Shops nearby?
- Is there a pharmacy in your neighborhood?
- Are there schools nearby?
- Are all these facilities and shops accessible via public transport? Etc.

As you will have discerned, the choice of location does not depend solely on the beauty of the neighborhood.

Unsurprisingly, good deals often cost more, so you need to tailor your requirements to your budget or learn to negotiate firmly and accept rejections.

Negotiating is an indispensable quality for a profitable real estate investor...

2.The profile of the rental property

In addition to the architecture of the property, the floor, the number of bedrooms and their layout, take into account the condition of the property in which you want to invest.

At this point, it is recommended to visit the accommodation time and time again and especially at different times of the day to evaluate the exposure of the housing to the sun, vis-à-vis or the state of the sound insulation.

Always be accompanied by a relative or a professional (usually a real estate expert) to detect defects and potential hidden defects of the property.

Do not hesitate to inform yourself precisely on the surface of the property which in this respect must be mentioned with exactitude in the preliminary contract as well as the authentic act.

This law does not apply to individual houses, pay attention.

In this case, also make sure of the existence of a damage insurance-book for any work done recently. This insurance will guarantee you compensation in case of poor workmanship.

Ask to visit the parking space or the cellar and make sure it is vacant and usable. A parking space can provide additional rental yield, being rented separately.

3.The immediate neighborhood

You would be wrong to neglect this point because a neighbor can make your life enjoyable as he can turn your day into hell. Even more, if you invest in a short-term rental.

4.Any work to do in your rental investment

Who supports the work?

The answer depends on the nature of the work that we summarize as follows:

Maintenance work on the building: ask the condominium syndicate

Generally (usually), apartments located in a condominium belong to the trustee who votes when maintenance needs to be done.

In this case, you must inquire of this trustee to know if work is already taking place or will take place later.

Resuming the previous general meeting PV condominium may allow you not to make a disastrous rental investment.

For example, if you have not seen in the PV that the facade of the building in which you want to invest will be redone and that this work not yet voted will be coupled with energy renovation from the outside ... Well, your financing plan may soon be flat!

Thus, if work has already been voted, it is up to the previous owner to cover their costs, but if they are in the process of reflection and the vote will take place when you own, it will be up to you to pay the amount required.

Do not hesitate to contact the condominium trustee to find out more, as some works can be costly and require that you advance a relatively large amount. Also, trustees are used to answering questions and usually do so without any language of wood

Last little trick, get the condo rules as soon as possible. If it includes a clause of bourgeois housing, go your way if you want to make seasonal furnished rental!

Over or under renovation cost.

Comprehending the degree of improvements a rental property need is essential to a compelling bargain. Real estate capitalists ought to aim to restore to the level of neighborhood market problems as well as understand that improvements can differ from neighborhood to area, even in the same city.

No matter the condition of the residential or commercial property, recognizing the extent of the improvement is a bespoke evaluation that requires emphasis. If all the residents in an area have ceramic tile kitchen counters, including granite kitchen counters, possibly wouldn't be a worthy investment as it would not cater to the standard occupant or owner in that community.

You might stay clear of over- or under-renovating by merely speaking with your team of regional professionals, including a real estate agent, residential or commercial property manager, professional, and so on. They are market professionals, as well as must have the ability to aid you in selecting worthwhile enhancements.

You can also explore other houses in the location when possible or utilize on the internet sources to see pictures and extent out the local competition. Doing your persistence before launching any improvement project may enhance your returns and shield you against losing time and also money on the wrong remodeling.

5.Learn about the rules of urban planning

This is fundamental, but still, too few investors learn before investing in rental real estate ... and we have nasty surprises AFTER the acquisition Not all municipalities have the same rules when it comes to construction, as it also depends on the neighborhood where your future rental investment is located. Expose your project to the urban planning department on which you depend, and try to find out if you can obtain a permit from the town hall or agglomeration.

Also, a small visit to the urban planning department of the area where you want to invest in rental real estate will allow you to get acquainted with new projects (a park, a shopping center, a leisure center, etc.) in the neighborhood. Or its surroundings. This can be extremely positive... or not!

6.The fiscal aspect of the transaction

When you are about to invest in rental real estate, whether new or old, you must, in addition to calculating the purchase price, take into account ancillary costs related to it, namely:

- Local taxes: housing taxes, garbage collection taxes, as well as the property tax;
- Registration fees: taxes paid to the State which represent 80% of notary fees.

For short-term furnished rentals, of course, the fees are higher:

7. The legal aspect of the transaction

You are not unaware that the passage to the notary is required to seal the transaction and that the presence of your lawyer is, in some cases, necessary.

It is essential to read the contract and understand exactly what it says at the risk of signing a sales agreement that is not in your favor. For example, you may inadvertently or ignorantly agree to cover co-ownership fees for work started before your acquisition of the property while it is up to the previous owner to pay for them.

8. The administrative aspect of the transaction and the borrower insurance

Make sure all your paperwork is in good standing and valid.

In case you need to make a loan, which is very strongly recommended to deduct the interest on loans and place your cash which will bring you elsewhere, do not hesitate to go around the banks to find the most advantageous rate.

Do not be surprised if the bank asks you to fill out a health questionnaire whose answers will determine the amount of your borrower insurance.

Some banks will even ask you for a complete medical examination, the results of which will determine their response.

See the right side of things: every 6 months, our insurance borrower pays us a complete check-up, we have iron health, and any failure will be detected very early.

9.Ask for the technical and energy diagnostic file.

This precaution is mainly reserved for investments in the former.

Pay attention to energy obsolescence, which decreases the value of the real estate by up to 35%

Unfortunately, the apartments you could buy do not always comply with current safety standards.

Well, we understand...

As a result, energy performance in the former is more moderate.

Do not hesitate to ask for the technical and energy diagnosis file so that you have a concept of the extent of the work to be done.

10.Estimate the total amount of the property you want to rent

The valuation of the total amount of the property is done by adding the price of the purchase to the additional expenses (notary fees, works, taxes ... etc.)

Once you have done the math, you have all the keys in hand to calculate a realistic rental yield and not veil your face!

How to beware of the mistake happens?

Educate on your own first.

If you're not familiar with the subtleties of real estate purchases, and also the real estate market you wish to purchase, become an expert before you set up any funding.

Depending upon the type of investment you intend to make—commercial or residential, house flipping or having as well as handling a building with tenants or perhaps temporary rentals-- obtain a full understanding of what's involved as well as whether you can manage it.

" It's great what they reveal on television, but there's a great deal of information as well as documents that come along keeping that. Which's where the mentoring and also partnering come right into play-- people can truly help you out," Tassell says.

Take your time.

Property is a significant financial investment, so do not make any choices until you feel positive in the deal.

In January, Wells Fargo launched a Wealth Planning Update, "Investing in Real Estate in Today's Market," which kept in mind that reduced interest rates in previous years have been critical to attracting financiers to real estate.

Seven months later, among the writers of the report, Scott Bennett, real estate advising expert for Wells Fargo Real Estate Asset Management, states the assumption that rates of interest would rise this year has transformed, as the Federal Reserve does not visualize enhancing rates in the immediate future. That gives financiers even more time to consider their choices meticulously.

" If anything, it's provided people the chance to look a little bit a lot more very closely at the chance they're thinking about since there's not this deadline of the rate of interest increasing," Bennett states. "We'll most likely remain in the reduced rate of interest atmosphere for the near term anyway."

Make connections.

Making the ideal friends can make a huge difference when you're beginning a brand-new company venture, which is why Tassell states connecting with a regional group or organization can assist you in surpassing fresh start with real estate investing. Close-by teams can usually be located via a search online, as well as they may have member charges in addition to non-member occasions.

Tassell has one warning, though: He suggests against single occasions by home turning or spending "experts" that use tricks of the profession; however no local understanding or constant aid.

"Those have a tendency to leave individuals with vacant pocketbooks and details they don't understand just how to execute, whereas a group supplies both education that requires time to answer the questions you really have, applies in your area, as well as typically you can develop mentoring as well as networking collaborations-- and those are crucial when you're going right into real estate," Tassell states.

Bennett also advises dealing with a certified real estate advisor. "It provides you a possibility to invest carefully, provides you an opportunity to spend alongside a specialist group, and it offers you a chance to learn the company along with a professional team whiles you're investing at the same time," he states.

Take into consideration the options.

Determine what sort of home possession will be best for your cash as well as where you ought to invest.

While purchasing buildings in your neighborhood market might feel like the best choice since you're familiar with the location, selecting an outside market might be much better for your lower line.

Peter Abualzolof, founder and also CEO of real estate financial investment information evaluation service Mashvisor, keeps in mind an investor from New York City who might not have the resources to spend in high-priced New York homes might concentrate on a smaller, less expensive market. It can suggest going into residential areas or noncoastal markets that are growing, such as Denver or Austin, Texas, where residential property is a bit much less pricey; however is seeing constant, substantial gains.

Put your eggs in other baskets.

Both before and during the investment process, watch on prices and your financial investments somewhere else. The one last thing you should do is place every little thing in you have right into a single real estate deal.

Bennett commonly works with Wells Fargo clients that have more significant profiles, with real estate functioning as a part of their overall investments. You must have differed investments outside of the real estate to assist balance out decreases in particular possession courses-- if real estate dives, as an example.

"We check out [real estate investment] as a possibility to branch out a profile," Bennett states.

Additionally, while short-term real estate investments like house flips might seem appealing, keeping real estate for more extended periods and also riding out missteps in the marketplace often tends to provide you far better protection in your financial investment.

Peter Abualzolof, founder as well as CEO of real estate investment data of evaluation solution Mashvisor, notes a financier from New York City who may not have the resources to invest in pricey New York buildings might concentrate on a smaller sized, much less expensive market. It might indicate going into suburban areas, or noncoastal markets that are growing, such as Denver or

Austin, Texas, where the property is a bit less costly yet is seeing regular, substantial gains.

Tips and advice for the investor.

Below's what a couple of skilled investors need to state concerning buying real estate via different market conditions and kinds of real estate markets.

Tips for newbies. The single essential initial step for aspiring real estate financiers is to figure out one's departure method, according to Andy Heller, writer of "Buy Low, Rent Smart, Sell High." There are instead a few alternatives; however, the two standard approaches are to get and hold rental or commercial properties as well as come to be a landlord or to come to be a flipper and ideally make a substantial profit upon the sale of the residential or commercial property.

For Heller directly, his service has thrived over the years with 3-year lease alternatives.

" You require to ask on your own what features will make that departure technique work. You require to acquire the right building to be successful," claims

Heller, who has focused on the Atlanta real estate market for years.

Like any financial investment, real estate investing needs an activity plan. "Once you determine your desire to scale it, it is necessary to consider the funds, the time, your debt and your lasting objectives to make sure that what you intend to do is attainable as well as realistic," Heller states.

His recommendation for novices is to sign up with a neighborhood investor's club as well as be familiar with individuals there. "It's uncommon that you can find somebody who can launch in real estate without some guidance. My guidance to a new investor would certainly be to sign up with an organization, discover experienced financiers, get them lunch as well as present your plan. Inquire about poking holes in it."

Scott Mednick, head of state of OCRE discussion forum, a real estate financier club, and also the founder of Marblehead Group Inc., concurs. He also has a caution for amateurs looking for information on how to get begun in the organisation.

" The opposite of the fence in this organisation is that individuals obtain drawn into these $40,000 to $50,000 boot camps," Mednick claims. "Don't do those. You're going to finish up purchasing things you don't need. If you're brand-new in business, the finest advice I can provide is to visit a local book shop and also review books on real estate investing. Discover the finest one or two publications and acquire those."

Tony Alvarez has operated in the Southern California real estate business for decades.

Alvarez claims all real estate investors are aiming for "that moment in time where we have built up sufficient income-producing assets to provide us with a comfortable requirement of living, despite economic problems or political nonsense."

For individuals new to real estate investing, Alvarez suggests initially figuring out which kind of real estate spending they desire to enter and why. Then they need to select a specific target market and examine it extremely. Next, established a goal, create a service strategy as well as develop systems to accomplish the wanted objective. Investors must take small, common-sense actions daily toward attaining that objective, such as speaking with vendors, proprietors and also neighborhood real estate professionals.

Tips for skilled investors. As for experienced investors, these long-time professionals have some sage guidance for them too. Heller's advice for seasoned investors might be unusual, particularly considering that these individuals are currently on top of their game.

" It's to remain modest," Heller says. In real estate, I see financiers all the time that believe they stroll on water.

Next, Heller states financiers must have lots of money deposited to function as a buffer of types. As soon as an investor has scaled bent on a more significant portfolio of residential or commercial properties, it is essential to have sufficient cash flow handy to refurbish 10 to 15 percent of those residential or commercial properties every year.

" Be prepared. Plan for the most effective, however get ready for the most awful," Alvarez recommends. "Insurance holds property security. Investors must ensure themselves as if the world is involving ruin them and insurance policy is their only defense."

In the long run, Alvarez claims real enemies to riches creation consist of greed, procrastination, laziness, imagined fears, as well as lack of information and also education and learning, among others.

From a flipper's viewpoint, Mednick states skilled experts require to stay concentrated on location and also price. "The finest suggestions are do not pay too much of what you're getting, because you'll obtain squeezed on the back end by customers," he suggests. "If you overpay and over rehab, you're not most likely to make the profit you require."

Buyers still want a bargain in this market, so they are pickier. They intend to see more properties as well as time is on their side so they are not shooting as quick. They wish to ensure they have a great location.

" I function a lot of different angles. I have a couple of real estate agents I have constructed connections with who call me when a deal is available. That assists me quite a little bit," Mednick says.

Along with constructing individual relationships with real estate experts, potential offers can be found making use of on-line resources such as the RealtyTrac.com and Auction.com, along with regional as well as national listing solutions.

Advice for all investors. To Heller, the most significant appeal of spending in real estate is that there are lots of methods to earn money by leveraging money-- whether it's the investor's own money or someone else's.

Be cautious; however he cautions since the same qualities that appeal to financiers can additionally be a capitalist's downfall. With real estate, the investors stand to lose more cash than he or she spent potentially. Still, Alvarez says bargains are always readily available.

If you're brand-new in the company, the best suggestions I can offer is to go to a neighborhood bookstore and read via books on real estate investing. For individuals brand-new to real estate investing, Alvarez recommends first establishing which kind of real estate investing they desire to get into and why. Investors must take tiny, common feeling steps daily toward achieving that goal, such as talking with sellers, owners and also local real estate experts

Chapter 7

Investment real estate: calculate correctly, choose meaningfully

Who wants to invest his money, often relies on the purchase of a rental property. But not every investment property is automatically lucrative and reliably raises high rental income. Many factors are crucial for a good return. How investors correctly calculate the purchase and find the right investment property.

An investment property can, at best, open up a long-term, lucrative source of income. In the worst case, however, it turns out to be a groschen grave.

Whether real estate is economically worthwhile as an investment depends above all on specific parameters. Interested parties must plan the financing and correctly calculate the purchase of the investment property. Here, location factors are just as crucial as the structural condition of the property.

Not every object is suitable for generating a good return. Even if a property looks good on paper: there are pitfalls that can get into the money. Therefore, acquirers should be aware of some criteria when they want to buy an investment property.

Find suitable investment property

Anyone who wants to buy an investment property should do so in a location with a future - that is, where unemployment is low, and the population does not shrink.

Buyers should also pay attention to the micro-location: A rundown property in a disreputable street is not a good deal. Conversely, an investment property in an average location may be the right choice if other factors fit: good condition, contemporary layouts, or good transport links indicate that the property may be of interest to many tenants.

The question as to whether substantial refurbishments will be made in the future also determines the attractiveness of an investment property: outdated building services or even building damage can lead to substantial follow-up costs; in the worst case, total refurbishment can cost even more than a new building. Also: The Energy Saving Ordinance (EnEV) even requires certain renovations. The costs incurred should also be taken into account.

Unusually high additional costs for the tenants can also speak against a particular investment property. Whether a property is well insulated and therefore requires little energy, or whether a lot of money for oil or gas must be spent, can be read from the energy certificate.

Even an attractive property can be a problematic investment namely if there are problem tenants in the house. Rental arrears, processes and subsequent evictions or even devastated apartments can go into the money. Therefore, buyers should carefully examine the tenant structure in the house: Particularly interesting in this context, whether there was in the past rent arrears, irregular rent payments or legal disputes with tenants.

Is the property overpriced or cheap? - The rental multiplier provides information

If an interesting investment property is found, its cost-effectiveness should be scrutinized more closely: The rent multiplier provides a first indication of whether a property tends to be cheap or expensive. The key figure can be easily calculated:

Multiplier = purchase price / annual cold rent

A property that costs 500,000 euros and incurs a rent of 25,000 euros per year has a multiplier of 20 because the purchase price would be generated with 20 annual cold rents. A multiplier of 40 would result in 12,500 euro rental income, a multiplier of 12.5 at 40,000 euro rental income.

For investment real estate in prime locations with anticipated rent increases, the multiplier of a multi-family house can ever be 40. In cities with high unemployment, declining population and growing vacancies, there are also properties whose multiplier is less than ten. The rental multiplier is therefore not an absolute size, which immediately gives information on whether an object is cheap or expensive. Rather, the more promising and future-proof a property appears, the higher may be this ratio.

Return and value of investment property

If the actual return on a property is to be calculated, net ratios are better than the multiplier. The formula for the net yield is:

Net yield (in%) = (annual rent - management costs) * 100 / (purchase price + purchase costs)

To determine generally whether the purchase price of an investment property is appropriate, the income capitalization method is suitable. For example, this also takes into account the value of the land without the property or the remaining expected useful life.

It should also be considered that burdens on an investment property can be detrimental to value. These include, for example, easements such as rights of way, housing rights or a social bond for the tenants. If the property is on a leasehold property, this is also depreciation.

This can be used to calculate future profitability and liquidity

Anyone who buys a top property with a high multiplier has indeed made a presumably future-proof investment, but should also remember its current liquidity.

Example calculation

A top apartment building in Munich costs two million euros. There are annual rental income expected from 50,000 euros. The rental multiplier, therefore, amounts to 40.

Assuming annual management costs of 5,000 euros, this results in a net rental income of 45,000 euros. With purchase costs of eight percent, a total of € 2,160,000 must be invested. The annual net return on the investment, in this case, is just under 2.1 percent.

If the buyer financed the entire purchase price including incidental costs with a bank loan with two percent interest and two percent initial repayment, the sum of the monthly installments would amount to 86,400 euros per year. The liquidity gap would be 41,400 euros.

On the safe side is, who can raise a part of the purchase price with equity and calculated so that the rental income is higher than the installment to be paid. Then there are reserves left for future repairs.

Tax aspects of investments

In addition to current rental income, tax aspects can also influence the return on an investment property.

On the one hand, the loan interest - but not the capital repayments - can be claimed for tax purposes. They reduce income, which reduces the individual tax burden. As the repayment portion of the loan installment continues to rise over time as the interest portion decreases, so does the tax savings over time.

On the other hand, an investment property can be depreciated for tax purposes as part of depreciation

(depreciation for wear and tear). There are different types of depreciation.

Investment property as a speculative object: The Treasury earns

If you consider an investment property as a short-term risky object, you must remember that there is a ten-year speculative period: capital gains must then be taxed at the individual income tax rate in the year in which they are earned. And not only that: the previously granted depreciations are summed up and also count as profit. An example: An investment property is sold after a few years holding time with a profit of 50,000 euros. During the holding period, the depreciation amounted to 30,000 euros. To tax in this case are 80,000 euros profit. Anyone who wants to avoid the taxation of speculative profits must, therefore, keep his investment property for more than ten years.

Self-test in the selection of investment property

Before the decision for or against a particular investment property falls, one should ask the question: Could I imagine using this property myself? It is not about the specific issue of whether you want to move in, but about whether you could imagine this from the tenant's perspective. Therefore, it is important to put yourself in the position of a typical prospective tenant: If I were in his position, would the property be interesting for me then? Those who get doubts about this self-test should think again about their investment plan.

Chapter 8

Why successful property capitalists will get even more do well?

Real estate investing is not as straightforward as getting a rental property and waiting for it to begin creating profits. Capable property investors not just spend their money, yet additionally their time and energy when it comes to real estate investing. Certain vital success factors need to be taken a right into account before purchasing a financial investment residential or commercial property and starting a spending career. Without more ado, it allows dive into the key aspects that every real estate investor should understand for a competent real estate spending job.

4 Key elements for a successful property investing career.

Success Factor # 1: Positive Capital

In real estate investing, favorable cash flow is the earnings made monthly from a rental property. The primary factor why positive cash flow is a vital success factor is simply that the higher the difference in between the rental earnings as well as the rental expenditures, the better the price of ROI. Successful residential property capitalists always look for favorable capital financial investment properties additionally since also when the property market is going down, the real estate capitalist would certainly still make cash through rental income till the economic climate recuperates. Favorable cash flow has a tendency to raise with time, permitting revenue property investors to make also more cash from real estate investing with each passing year.

In enhancement, positive cash flow pays for a real estate investor's property loan, which result in boosting the earnings building's equity! Not only that, but successful property investors can save the additional income from favorable cash flow to make use of as down payment to acquire another investment property. Hence, positive cash flow is a crucial success variable in real estate investing because it permits income real estate investors to buy as well as possess several investment properties!

Success Factor # 2: Financial Analysis

Another critical success considers real estate investing is carrying out a monetary analysis and also recognizing the monetary elements of possessing a rental property. There are various funding approaches for purchasing an investment building-- there are a mortgage, private money lending institutions, tough money loan providers, etc. Successful property capitalists continuously assess the needs as well as outcomes of each technique before choosing exactly how to fund their financial investment residential properties.

Various other points, a real estate investor needs to be acquainted with include: rental real estate tax, repayment strategies, as well as mortgage computation. For effective real estate investing, constantly identify your current monetary circumstance, your individual financial goals, and the optimum amount of financing for which you are eligible, and also set a budget plan before buying an investment residential property, so you do not locate on your own financially distraught.

Success Factor # 3: Rental Strategy

Some income property financiers decide for the traditional rental approach since they think about Airbnb rentals too high-risk as well much work. What determines which rental method is the finest is the location of your rental property.

The reason why establishing the rental strategy is a success consider real estate investing is that the rental plan will eventually influence your price of return on financial investment. As an example, when purchasing a residential rental property in a location with the stable tourism industry, productive real estate investors would purchase an Airbnb (temporary) leasing because it would undoubtedly produce higher returns than a standard (long-lasting) service.

Success Factor # 4: Property Management

Excellent Property management is an additional essential success factor in real estate investing. Managing a revenue property requires time, company, social abilities, and interest in details. By residential property administration, we don't imply finding occupants and collecting a monthly rental fee. As a real estate investors, you require to identify the most excellent way to advertise your financial investment property, along with performing a lessee testing procedure to find the most active tenants-- the optimal renter is one who pays the monthly rental fee and also doesn't harm the rental building.

Additionally, residential property management calls for an investor to monitor repairs, keep the rental building, and manage any concerns occupants may have. As a real estate capitalist, if you don't have the moment and power required for property administration, then real estate investing is possibly not the most effective profession choice for you.

Expert property investors always look for real cash flow streaming investment properties additionally because also when the real estate market is going down, the real estate investor would certainly still make cash through rental revenue until the economic situation recovers. Hence, positive cash flow is a crucial success aspect in real estate investing because it permits earnings property financiers to purchase as well as have several financial investment buildings!

As a real estate investor, you require figuring out the best way to promote your investment residential or commercial property, in enhancement to conducting a lessee testing procedure to locate the finest lessees-- the perfect occupant is one who pays a month-to-month rental fee and also doesn't harm the residential rental property.

An alternative to property management and best real estate investing is working with a specialist residential property monitoring! There are numerous expert property management companies (such as Pillow), which are experienced in taking care of residential investment properties and offer a set of solutions to residential property financiers consisting of marketing, funding, occupancy, repair services, and also upkeep.

10 Behaviors of Effective Real estate Investors

Specific universities give training and also courses that primarily help real estate clients; a degree is not necessarily a qualification to profitable real estate investing. Whether a capitalist has a degree or even certainly not, there are specific qualities that cover real estate investors typically have. Below are the 10 Behaviors that strongly efficient real estate investors share.

1. Create a Plan

Property investor needs to approach their real estate activities as a business to set up and obtain brief- and also lasting objectives. A company strategy also makes it possible for entrepreneurs to picture the big photo, which assists sustain concentrate on the goals as opposed to any kind of minor setbacks. Real estate investing could be made complex as well as demanding, and strong planning may keep entrepreneurs organized as well as on duty.

2. Know the marketplace

Helpful real estate investors acquire extensive expertise in their chosen market(s). Following existing styles, consisting of any kind of modifications in customer spending practices, property mortgage, and the joblessness cost, to name a few, lets real estate clients accept current circumstances and prepare for the future. It allows all of them to anticipate when trends may change, generating prospective possibilities for the prepared financier.

3. Be Honest

Real estate capitalists are often not obligated to promote a specific degree of ethics. It will be straightforward to take conveniences of this situation, most effective real estate capitalists preserve higher reliable criteria. Because real estate putting in involves people, an investor's online reputation is probably to be extensive. Efficient investor recognizes it is better to become decent, as opposed to seeing what they can quickly getaway along with.

4. Establish a Niche

Investors must develop a concentration if you want to gain the intensity of know-how vital to becoming successful. Putting in the time to construct this amount of understanding of a specific place is important to long-term effectiveness. When a particular market is mastered, the investor can quickly go on to added locations using the same in-depth method.

5. Promote Referrals

Suggestions generate a massive part of a real estate financier's company, so investors must alleviate others with respect. Successful real estate clients pay for interest to information, listen closely and also react to problems as well as concerns, and also represent their business in a favorable and qualified fashion.

6. Keep Educated

As along with any company, it is important to remain up to date along with the legislations, guidelines, language, and fads that develop the manner of the property investor's business. Investors that drop responsible for risk certainly not only shedding drive in their organisations yet additionally legal implications if regulations are overlooked or even damaged. Effective real estate investors stay taught and adjust to any type of regulative changes or economic patterns.

7. Recognize the Risks

Inventory or also futures market capitalists are swamps with alerts regarding the integral dangers included in trading. Investors nevertheless, are most likely to find promotions declaring merely the reverse: that it is effortless to generate cash in real estate. Sensible real estate investors comprehend the threats-- not just concerning real estate offers yet additionally the legal effects included-- and readjust their organisations to minimize those risks.

8. Acquire an Accountant

Taxes make up a substantial portion of a property investor's yearly costs. Comprehending present tax obligation legislations may be complicated and require time far from the business at the palm. A pointy property investor keeps the companies of a qualified, trusted accounting professional to deal with your business's manuals. The prices linked with the accountant may be negligible when contrasted to the financial savings a professional can easily give business.

9. Find Help

Learning the real estate spending business is testing for somebody seeking to perform traits by themselves. Helpful investors commonly associate aspects of their success to others, whether it is an advisor, legal representative, or supportive buddy. Somewhat than risk money and time handling complicated trouble alone, productive real estate investors recognize it deserves the added expenses (in conditions of amount of money and vanity) to welcome various other individuals' proficiency.

10. Build a Network

A network may offer essential help as well as create options for both brands new and also seasoned real estate investors. This form of a team consisted of a well-chosen coach, service partners, clients, or even participants of a non-profit institution, allows capitalists to test and support one another. Because a lot of real estate putting in relies on experiential learning, sensible investors recognize the usefulness of creating a system.

Whether an entrepreneur has a degree or certainly not, there are specific features that top real estate clients typically possess. Real estate investors need to approach their real estate activities as a service in purchase to establish and accomplish quick- as well as long-lasting objectives. Suggestions create a massive portion of a real estate client's service, so real estate investors must alleviate others along with appreciation. Smart real estate investors understand the dangers-- not merely in phrases of real estate offers but likewise the legal effects involved-- as well as change their companies to reduce those threats.

Because much of real estate investing counts on empirical understanding, intelligent real estate clients know the importance of constructing a system.

Chapter 9

Cases study

Sustainability is more important than growth.

I have been selling land and projects to real estate investors for several years, and I have realized that for a couple of years the sustainable development of buildings has been demanded now. Sustainable development projects, because saving energy and caring for the environment is what most attracts the final buyers. This is not a trend; It is a trend that will increasingly go.

Investors prefer this type of real estate development that, in the long run, is more profitable. If you are a property developer and you are searching for capitalists for your task, you will find them much more easily if you have applied sustainable development to your project.

The real estate investors institutional (and some private) have found a formula that allows them to increase their profits, not substantially, but quickly offering ecological houses; that is to say that they save energy and help the sustainable development of the community. The sale of real estate products with energy savings and built with materials that do not harm the environment has skyrocketed in the last three years.

The plaintiffs or buyers of a house or a house built from sustainable development, have a high buyer profile, which means for fast real estate investors and good benefits. The sustainable real estate development in addition to giving prestige makes money. The buyer is willing to pay a plus for green homes.

True, we are all concerned about improving our environment, but not everyone has the possibility of acquiring a home, demanding that it be a sustainable home. It does not matter, the real estate investor or knows who can and wants to pay this extra for buying a house that improves their quality of life and is all or part ecological.

"Real estate investors with this" sustainable "profile seek to invest or be partners in luxury real estate projects, with prices above $ 7000. 000 to be able to reach that buyer of high purchasing power who cares about the social image that his new ecological home provides him. "

The promoters know that part of the problem of being successful with new development is sales. Continuous sales are needed from the first moment to be able to continue building with tranquility and that works are not delayed.

It should not be like that. This business model where buyers finance the work with their reserves and monthly payments is obsolete and will be used less and less. Yes, if today many new promotions are sold like this in pre-sale; but it is already showing to sell real estate in this way and tend not to deliver the homes on the promised date.

Real estate investors do not want to sell with this formula. They want to sell fast and well, and they know how to do it. For this reason, they prefer to associate with sustainable development projects because the real estate buyer of today is sensitive to this issue.

Residential real estate projects that can be traded on a flat or pre-sale basis and built with a sustainable development base and located in a protected environmental zone are also in the spotlight of these real estate investors. The sale of these "green" real estate products are easier to market since there is a social awareness towards respect for the environment.

Increasingly buyers of homes with high purchasing power care about the environment in which they live as they are very aware that this environment influences their well-being and has a direct impact on the environment.

When a financially stable life is reached, quality of life is sought, and the natural resources are taken advantage of.

"On the other hand, the cost of building each real estate unit in a project built on a sustainable basis, (essentially with energy savings and with the use of materials that have been recycled or do not contain certain products), is not much more expensive. And this is well known by real estate investors. "

Real estate investors seek to partner with developers or builders who offer them a product of sustainable development because they know how to capture the right customer quickly. His strategy, in 3 steps to roughly is the following, (I have seen it several times, and in 2 of them I have been personally involved):

1. Once they have become partners of the developer, usually with a significant amount of capital, their first concern is to prepare the land; that is, to urbanize the land that will generally be in a condominium, residential or subdivision.

2. Once the urbanization phase is complete, it is when the marketing campaign is launched. This is the key. If you start marketing before you have the full development, you will lose many potential sales and the launch of the "new" project will lose much of its effect.

I repeat, marketing a new promotion before the urbanization phase is a mistake. Those who are against this approach argue that they have come 10 or 20 units in this way. I tell them: assuming that this figure was right, they could have sold three times as many units if they had launched the promotion after the urbanization of the land. This is proven!

NOTE: I must point out that putting a promotion as soon as possible in the market is mostly driven and encouraged by the banks that give credit to developers and real estate marketing to know very little.

3. Real estate investors prepare the launch campaign very well. They use Public Relations, social networks, and online promotion at the same time, all supported by a website adapted specifically for the commercialization of sustainable development housing to get the information requests that are generated.

A real estate product of sustainable development must be known to promote it to the right people and not to everyone who has the money to acquire one. This is another common mistake that promoters make. The right approach is to reach the ideal client.

For this reason, real estate investors, even if they invest in another country, always contact specialized advisors with experience in selling this type of real estate product.

A real estate investor knows that the presentation of a sustainable development product is the basis for attracting qualified stakeholders.

To be able to sell first you have to capture the appropriate information requests or "leads" by various means. This is achieved first with a website with specific content and then with a campaign that is congruent with the content of the website. Let's say that the promotional message leaves the content of the website.

This website should contain, among others, the following:

1. A Quality Report or Technical Specifications with clear and simple text.

2. Description of each type of property with text between 800 -1,000 words to position the page online and in social networks. It is accompanied by images and a 2D plane.

3. Form of payment and security of payments, (trust). Clearly, show the payment method with examples and explain how the amounts deposited in accounts are secured. Some promoters argue that this information should be given in people. This is not like this. The goal is to get requests for information, and this explanation helps to get enough. In other words, what you are doing is to generate credibility and transparency.

4. Plans, images, and specifications in downloadable files on the website. All a list that can be downloaded, you

have to give all the information possible. Also, all this information will be used in your online promotion campaigns.

5. A Blog that will serve to position each of the pages of the website in search engines and Facebook.

6. Explanation of how sustainable development applies to each dwelling: how housing saves energy, what materials have been used for this energy-saving, why valuable materials help to maintain the environment, how manufactured furniture has been with recycled materials, etc.

It must be demonstrated to the potential buyer that the real estate product offered is "sustainable". Generally, this is achieved with a free download guide from the website and Facebook.

To always attract the best real estate investors who participate in your business, always think about sustainability. Introduce them to a sustainable development project, and you will get financing sooner than you think.

Moreover, some financial entities or investment groups offer incentives to real estate investors who decide to put their money into projects that, as a financial entity, offer them, not only profitability but an additional prestige that they will later use in their relationship campaigns. Public.

The financial sector has been uploaded to the car of sustainable development for some time, and some real estate developers have not yet realized it. Do not be one of them.

How can you present your project to real estate investors?

You must prepare an Informative Dossier that contains all the project information which clearly explains the phases of the project, the total cost of the project, the stages of realization of the project, the type of company or association that is expected with the new partner and an analysis of rentability d where it is demonstrated that the project is viable and profitable.

For example, if the project requires an investment of $ 12.3 million, detail where those $ 12.3 million will be invested and then demonstrate how much will be earned before taxes and how long. For this, you need to present an estimate of monthly sales.

In reality, what you do is present a business plan that he, with more experience than you, will modify and improve. The real estate investor wants to see where the profitability of his money is if he decides to invest.

Demonstrate to the real estate investor where the business opportunity is and how much each partner will earn based on their percentage of participation in the company.

Every real estate product built from the base of sustainable development sells quickly because there is demand. As a developer or builder, you have the project and the real estate investor the capital and experience in the sale of this product. A perfect tandem if you find the right investor. Cheer up! There are thousands of capitalists out there ready to purchase this kind of project.

In conclusion

Investing in the real estate market is an excellent option, as it is always growing. A simismo offers different options of accessible investments to all the capitals, ages, and needs.

These alternatives range from the purchase of a department and the mixed-use of properties to the investment in land plots for future buildings.

Your alternatives as a real estate investor are many, but it depends on your objectives if they are profitable or not for you.

Finally, if you liked the book, I would like to ask you to do me a favor and leave a review for the book on Amazon. Just go to your account on Amazon or click on the link below.

CLICK HERE TO LEAVE A REVIEW ON AMAZON!

Thank you and good luck!